BUILDING WITH A STORM IN MIND

FAITH TO SURVIVE

FOREWORD BY JOHN H. WALKER

TOBIAS M. WALL

Published By:
Jasher Press & Co.
www.jasherpress.com
customerservice@jasherpress.com
1.888.220.2068
P.O. Box 14520
New Bern, NC 28561

Copyright© 2014
Interior Text & Cover Design by Jasher Press
Istockphoto

ISBN: 978-0692268223

All rights reserved. Except for brief excerpts used in reviews, no portion of this work may be reproduced or published without expressed written permission from the author or the author's agent.

First Edition
Printed and bound in the United States of America

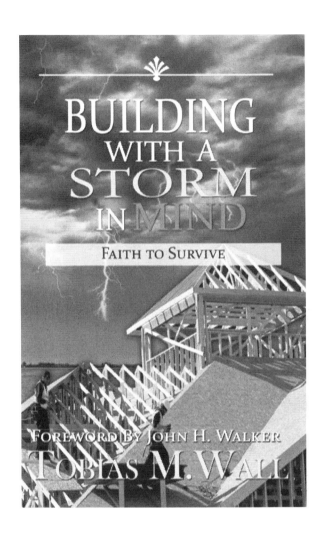

JASHER PRESS & CO.

You can't predict the future. You can't undo past mistakes. Though past mistakes form regrets, they can turn into experiences. It is only after being through a storm that you can truly appreciate the sunshine.

Dedication

I dedicate this book to the woman that gave me life and in turn gave me back to God at an early age. My mother, Doris Wall-Marshall, has weathered many storms in her life: the loss of a husband, the loss of her parents, and has battled sickness. She has always been like a tree planted by the rivers of water: she is strong, firm, and rooted. Thank you mom, for always trusting in the God in me, being my biggest cheerleader, my #1 fan, and never giving up on me. I love you eternally, Mom. You are the best!

INTRODUCTION

I greet you in the sovereign name of Jesus Christ. Recently, in the United States we have experienced a great deal of storms that have battered the East Coast, as well as, the Gulf Coast. It has been indicated that the U.S. Government and other engineers knew that the levees that protected the shore lines of Louisiana, Mississippi, and Alabama were not equipped to handle storm surges that could have the power of a Hurricane Katrina. Yet, no one did anything to make the situation better. In the body of Christ there is something that warns us of the coming storms..... The Bible declares in *John 16:33, "I have told you these things, so that in me you may have {perfect} peace and confidence. In the world you will have tribulation and trials and distress and frustration; but be of good cheer for I have overcome the world."*

Let me take this time to dispel any rumors that being a Christian gives you a ticket to easy street. No! My brothers and sisters life is not a bed of roses. It does not matter if you walk around with a pulpit Bible under your arm or a big cross around your neck; storms are still coming. It doesn't matter if you drive a Lexus or a Bentley, if you live in a mansion or in a penthouse; there's a storm with you in mind.

This book will not give you a quick 1, 2, 3, easy guide in avoiding storms. It will not give you a short cut around life's storms; however, it will show you a Godly and biblical fashion of how to build your faith with a storm in mind. I pray that this book will help you on your Christian journey that lies ahead. It is a fact that there are storms out on the ocean of life, which are Category 5 hurricanes and some are small thunderstorms. Whatever category storm you face, arm yourself with the Word of God, so that you will be able to stand the storms of time.

Table of Contents

Introduction	9
"My Life's Storms"	17
"Build on the Rock"	27
"Thank God for what he didn't do"	35
"I did survive"	43
"I can't take no more"	49
"I am an Eagle"	57
"Don't Ever Give up"	63
About the Author	73

Acknowledgements

The peerless Texas preacher, the late Dr. A. Louis Patterson, once said, "Every man living is either in a storm, headed for a storm, or just coming out of a storm." Pastor Tobias Wall offers us wisdom from the reservoirs of his life about how we should face our storms. From the challenges that have changed his life, he shares his greatest test, but also his greatest testimonies of the victories that he has experienced through a well-founded faith in Jesus Christ. It will be a tremendous blessing and benefit to all of us who listens receptively to the offerings of this pastor, preacher, and teacher who shares invaluable lessons for abundant living. I pray that each of us will attempt to steady ourselves in these timid times and will remember to build with the storm in mind.

J.A. McFarlan
Macedonian Baptist Church
Cheraw, South Carolina

Foreword

I have been in ministry for over three decades and have authored five books. I am so honored to have been asked to write the foreword for such a great work. Through my many years of serving God's people, I have witnessed the various storms in their lives. I have learned that Christians are like ships that will sooner or later have to face the tempest. In the dock, it is in safety and for months it goes on building and adding on planks, riveting them together, so that the water shall not get in between them. Then the machinery and fittings are added, and it all goes out into the harbor, and then upon the water to see whether she is watertight. She only goes out after all of this is done and is able to defy the tempest and the storms because she was "built with a storm in mind. "

Pastor Tobias Wall has given a blueprint on how to build our lives, while preparing for a storm. I have known Pastor Wall for over 20 years. I have witnessed first-hand his love and passion for God's people. His ministry exemplifies his unselfishness in helping God's people to fulfill their divine destiny. He is one that was born out of due season and is beyond his time. His cutting edge ministry and his 21st century leadership qualifies him for such an arduous task of teaching, preaching, and equipping God's people.

Tobias allows us to look through his window of more than 18 years of surviving various storms. "Building with a Storm in Mind" is a book that every saint must carry on their journey of life. This book not only addresses your storms, but gives the reader a step by step process on how to navigate the storm and survive them.

I commend Pastor Wall for unveiling himself and sharing with the kingdom citizens. "Building with a Storm in Mind" must be read by both the pulpit and the pew. There is a commonality that helps the reader see that God has a purpose and plan for your storm. Each chapter will take you deeper and deeper in understanding the awesome power of God and His ability to take care of you and restore you in spite of life's uncertainties. Thank you Pastor for your transparency and the hope you give the reader that no matter what, God's people are survivors.

On a personal note I want to thank you for having the audacity to write such a book. I have faced my share of storms in my personal life and through ministry. After reading your book I am more confident and convinced that the prophet Nahum's words in Nahum 1:3 are forever true:

"The Lord hath his way in the whirlwind and in the storm and the clouds are the dusts of his feet."

"Building with a Storm in Mind" will certainly be placed in my arsenal as I continue teaching, preaching, and equipping God's people.

John H. Walker D. Min, Senior Pastor
Macedonia Baptist Church
Charlotte, NC

Chapter 1

"MY LIFE'S STORMS"

At this very moment and instance, I'm facing one of the most powerful storms I have ever faced. It's been 8 months this time around. This has been the longest time that my dad has ever stayed in the hospital. Several years ago, my dad was diagnosed with Lung Disease and became very ill. I guess at this point I should at least tell you who my dad is; he is the greatest dad in the entire world. He is Pastor William Thomas Wall Jr. He is a native of Wadesboro, N.C., married to my mom, Doris Wall, and the father of three children, Phyllis, Tobias, and Theo.

It's early in the morning, Tuesday, October 4, 2005, as the sun rises over the trees, the rays of the sun breaks through the curtains, and fills the room. My mother and I sat next to the hospital bed in the Medical Intensive Care Unit (MICU) at Mercy Hospital in Charlotte, North Carolina.

My Life's Storms

Yesterday, October 3, 2005, my father was taken off life support. My father, dad, hero, and best friend's life is passing from his body right before my eyes. I'm trying to hold back the tears, while staring at the monitor. I feel like a little boy looking out the window with anticipation for his father to return home. His blood pressure is dropping by the moment and it feels like my heart is skipping a beat, as his pressure drops. Helpless, I begin to call his name over and over again, hoping and praying that he would miraculously open his eyes and we can all go home. I needed my dad to hear the tremble in my voice that now sounds like a small child who is afraid of the creeps he hears in the night. I needed him to hear me and open his eyes. It never happened...

I questioned God. I was even angry with Him. I needed to know, "Why My Father?" All these other people in this world and God chose, "my father." I've never seen him drink, curse, or even say one unkind word to my mother. He has always been kind and humble. He always taught us to be good to one another. He always showed us how to love everybody and be kind enough to say, "thank you." He's never pastored a large church, but he had a heart after God. I remember dad staying up day after day studying for sermons and waiting on God to lead him in the right direction. Dad was and will always be the greatest definition of what a pastor should be. He not only preached the Word of God, but he lived the Word every day of his life.

At the age of 35, it is hard to believe that I have had a lot of storms in my life, but this storm by far is the storm that has shaken the foundation of my soul. The man that showed me how to fish, drive, cut grass, chop wood, and even talked to me about the birds and the bees, was slipping away right before my eyes. Again, I am focused on the monitor; it's getting harder to look, but my eyes are staring at it. I can see through my swollen eyes that are full of tears that his vital signs are steadily dropping. My stomach is in knots, my hands are dripping sweat, and I am fighting to hold back the tears. I'm trying to stay strong for my mom, but instead of being a 35-year-old adult sitting with his parents; I am now like a child praying to hear dad's voice.

I teach and preach about faith all the time. At our ministry, we always stand on **Hebrews 11:1 which says; "Now faith is the substance of things hoped for and the evidence of things not seen."** It's in this very moment that my faith must withstand this storm. Faith is the ability to trust *God's* Word in every situation that you are facing in life. Faith is the assurance or the title deed of things hoped for. Just like a title deed is evidence of real estate, your faith is evidence of your eternal estate in God.

It's now 9:00am and I'm still in the MICU. I've just called my uncle John, who is on his way to the hospital. While I'm still staring at the monitor, dad's blood pressure is now down to 70/40. His heart rate dropped to 42 and his oxygen level is 40. I begin to realize that dad's time is almost up. My heart is racing. In my mind I start remembering the old days. On my 16th birthday, dad took me to get my driver's license. I remember clearly that it was drizzling on that morning. Dad told me to remember what he had taught me. He said, "Just do what I've taught you and everything would be ok." Everything was ok because I received my driver's license that day and then later after school dad took me to the car dealership. When we got there, dad saw a green Honda with 4 doors. He asked, "Do you like this car." I said "yes." He said, "Happy 16th Birthday!" The memory fades and I snap back into reality. My eyes are now filled with tears, but still glued to the monitor; the lump in my throat makes it hard to swallow. It's only been 16 minutes, but it feels like forever. It is 9:16 am and mom is comforting dad to assure him that, "all is well." Lovingly, she rubs his head, as she too realizes that time is not long and that things are not good.

    I held his hand tight, knowing that this is probably the last time I'll get to hold his hand on this side of Heaven. Though I am heartbroken that dad is slipping away, I'm confident that he will be in a far greater place. I prayed for peace of mind and God granted it.

Psalms 23 says; "Yea thou I walk through the valley of the shadow of death I will fear no evil; for thou art with me thy rod and thy staff comfort me." The Word of God comforted me. I knew that God would hold me in the hollow of His hand. I needed to feel the very presence of God right then, more than ever before. My knees got weak, my stomach dropped, and tears that I could no longer hold back streamed down my face. The more I tried to hold back the tears, the more they flowed. Suddenly, the room became still.... all of his vital signs dropped and the very sign of life was gone. Frantically, my mother calls out his name, while being weak, and with an agonizing disbelief she nearly fainted. My parents had 36 years of marriage and what was seemingly a sweet life. A marriage unlike any other, day after day he made her dreams come true. He was her partner, friend, and love; the man she vowed to never part until this very moment. He supported her through the openings of two businesses; Noah's Arc and Noah's Arc Too and made it possible for her to go back to school. It is now 9:32 a.m., merely 16 more minutes have gone by and my father has slipped away. There is stillness in the room. I now know the stillness I felt was an assurance. A knowledge that I have of believing that being absent from the body is to be present with the Lord.

He looks so peaceful now, like a bird that has been freed from captivity. Uncle John has just arrived, but he was a moment too late. The monitor that I have stared at all day has just been silenced by the nurse. Husband, father, brother, and friend now rest in eternal peace. Our lives will never be the same. A void will always be there; an emptiness that can never be replaced.

It has been stated that the center of the storm is where you will find the most peace. Jesus has given me that peace. It surpasses all understanding. At this moment, another level of responsibility has been given to me. It is now my sad duty to make calls and repeatedly say the words that haunt me even now: Dad has passed away. Among my calls I notify my brother Theo, my sister Phyllis, Smith Funeral Home, and Senior Deacon Mr. Clarence Rorie. I ask that all church members are made aware of his passing. After saying it so many times, I know I need to cry. I've been trying not to break down, but it's getting harder to remain strong. It hurts, but I know we will be alright. Dad has shown us who to lean and depend on.

In the following days, people came by to support us. Family, friends, neighbors, and church members stopped by with food daily. We had food for days. The love and kindness shown to us was wonderful and we were forever grateful.

Mr. H.C. Smith, Director of the Funeral home called, to let us know that dad was ready to be seen. I looked down at him dressed, so peacefully in his red and white robe, he looks great. Dad looks like himself, but only asleep. It's hard for my mother. She begins to weep for the absence of her soul mate. Though she misses him, in her heart she knows they shall meet again.

The time is drawing closer, its Friday morning, the day before the funeral. I tossed and turned all night struggling to sleep. I stopped trying, so at 6:00 a.m. I got up and decided to drive out to Olive Branch. I am blessed to have been called to pastor Olive Branch Missionary Baptist Church in Marshville, NC. I went into the office to try and gather my thoughts. I was asked by my father to do his eulogy. I've been thinking and praying about what to say. A million things have crossed my mind. I went to the sanctuary and sat in the center seat in the pulpit. Suddenly, I was clear and I began to thank God for blessing us with such a wonderful and honest dad. I will never be able to tell you all that he has meant to us. Even now, we know that God loved him more.

I needed a comfort that only the Holy Spirit could grant, courage that only Jesus could provide, and strength that could only come through faith.

The Bible tells us in *II Corinthians 12:9 (abr.) His strength is made perfect in our weakness.* I pray God strengthens me where I'm weak and build me up where I'm torn down. I need a Word from the Lord.

It's Saturday, October 9, 2005, the day of the funeral. Everyone is on pins and needles. Friends and family members are arriving from all parts of the United States. I closed the bedroom door to get a moment of silence. I had looked and searched for the perfect passage of Scripture for this moment. Then it happened: *John 13:15 says; "For I gave you an example that you also should do as I did to you."* It defines the life of my father. The funeral cars arrived. There were six long silver limousines to drive us to the place where I would deliver words of comfort and the time was drawing near. It was the longest ride of my life. Pulling up, I noticed cars lined up everywhere. People we hadn't seen in ages had come to show respect to our Dad.

Dad liked to hear my brother sing, so in honor of Dad, Theo sang one of Dad's favorite songs. It was amazing. He sung "Pray on my Child." The spirit was high. The home going celebration was beautiful. There were remarks by pastors and friends that talked about dad's humbleness, loyalty, and faithfulness towards God and his fellow man. There must have been over 700 people packed in the chapel. When the songs, prayers, and remarks were over; it was time for me to eulogize my father. I talked briefly from the subject "Like Father, Like Son." One of the greatest compliments that can be given to a child is that you look like your parents. People often said that I looked just like "Tom," my dad. I appreciate that now more than I ever did before. He always told me and my brother to never let our family name go down. Now, I know that he didn't just only mean the "Wall" family name, but the family name of God. It was at that point when I delivered the message that I felt a shift in my spirit. God had taken me to another level. Somehow, I had received a double portion of the anointing. My mind was richer, my spirit felt stronger, and my desire for His Word had grown. The power to preach the Gospel had increased.

I understand that storms will come. Your race, gender, and status don't matter. Just as sure as a man is born, he will one day die. This one road, we all must face. You must never forget that this world is not our home. We are just pilgrims passing through. Don't get too attached to the things of this world, for this is only our temporary residence. The only thing that will keep you in the midst of any storm is to be rooted and grounded in the Word of God.

CHAPTER 2

"BUILD ON THE ROCK"

Matthew 7:24-27, we see there are two types of hearers. They are represented in their true characters. We have the opportunity to look at two types of builders in Matthew 7, as well. One was wise for he built his house on the rock and the other one was foolish for he built his house upon sand. For the foolish one, there is a rock provided for him to build his house upon and that rock is Christ. He is our hope. The church "Ecclesia" is built upon the rock of Jesus the Christ. The Bible says, in ***Matthew 16:16 (abr.) Simon Peter answered and said, "Thou art the Christ, the Son of the living God."*** Jesus in return blesses Peter by saying the things in which you have said was not revealed to you by flesh in blood, but this truth comes from God. Jesus said, "You are Peter (Petros, a little rock) and upon this rock (Petra, a big rock) I will build my church."

Upon himself, the rock of ages living stone, the Precious "corner stone" a stone of stumbling and a rock of offense.

Christ is the sure foundation of His church and all believers are little building stones into the Holy Temple of the Lord. Matthew 7 deals with two types of builders; one wise and one foolish. When one builds upon a rock he must first make the preparation for the storm. Local weather channels give safety tips to help us prepare for storms. They give you suggestions to protect you from lightning, flash floods, ice storms, heat strokes, hurricanes, and tornadoes. Just like the weather channel gives us things that we need to survive in the natural. There are things that we need to survive in the spiritual.

Batteries-Energizer uses the slogan that their batteries "keeps going and going and going..." In other words they will outlast all others. The Bible says, in ***Psalm 125:1 "Those who trust in, lean on, and confidently hope in the Lord are like Mount Zion, which cannot be moved but abides and stands fast forever."*** In the body of Christ we need to possess the spirit of the energizer battery. We must have a spirit of endurance. Endurance is the ability to keep on going in spite of adverse situations. Let me admit to you, it is hard to keep going when you feel your foundation has been shaken. The simplest thing for the believer to do is to throw in the towel, tuck his tail between his legs, and go hide. The Bible says, in ***II Timothy 1:7 "For God hath not given us the spirit of fear, but of power and of love and of a sound mind."*** Satan wants us to believe that God will leave us in time of trouble. Satan is as a roaring lion; however, he's only a mouse with a megaphone. We as the body of Christ must take God at His Word and understand that we have an everlasting power through Christ Jesus that will never fail. We must endure this race. It's not about giving in and giving up, but about holding up and holding on under the pressures of this world. Storms will come, but hold on. You will face battles, but stay the course. Trials and temptations will come every day in your life, but in the name of Jesus hold onto the hand of God.

<u>Flash Light</u>- Matthew *5:16 says; "Let you light shine before men that they may see your good deed and praise your father in heaven."* When I was growing up there was a little song that we use to sing entitled "This Little Light of Mine." The song says, "*This little light of mine, I'm going to let it shine. This little light of mine, I'm going to let it shine. This little light of mine, I'm going to let it shine. Let it shine, let it shine, let it shine. Everywhere I go; I'm going to let it shine."* As Christians we need to let our light shine. We have to understand that people see the light of Jesus through us. They see it through our character and our integrity. We are the 67 books of the Bible. The only Bible some people will ever read is your life. The light of Jesus cannot shine through a person that shouts on Sunday and by Monday they are in the break room cracking jokes. The world needs to see Jesus through us. Suicide is at an all-time high. We are living in a world that has become dark and gloomy; people are looking for someone to lift them up out of their dark place. It is a mandate by God to share the love of Jesus to someone else. We should not have a selfish salvation. We should not only want to see others saved, but we should be a flash light that helps light their path to Jesus. We may not be able to tell everyone, but we can tell someone about the love of Jesus.

Rope (Faith) - *Hebrews 11:1 says; "Now faith in the substance of things hoped for and the evidence of things not seen."* Faith is the title deed to your eternal life. The Bible declares in *Hebrews 11:6 (abr.) without faith it is impossible to please God.* Faith says to trust God when you can't trace Him. Faith says sacrifice and don't worry about the outcome. Faith allows us to start walking and ask questions later. Faith is God's Word in action.
The key to success in the Christian life is the same as it was for Christ and the heroes of our faith.

Spiritual success is found in the ability to endure. In *Hebrews 12:3, we read how we are to consider Christ who "endured" such contradiction of sinners against himself lest ye be wearied and faint in your mind.* If there is one character flaw that we should be without, it would be that of a quitter. A Christian should never quit. We are admonished over and over again to endure. When believers build on the rock of Jesus Christ we can stay in the fight to the very end. We can overcome and endure all things that come our way.

Water- What is water? Water is a transparent, odorless, tasteless fluid that forms the seas, lakes, rivers, and rain. It is the basis of the fluids of living organisms. Water is something that many people take for granted and it is very important to one's survival. It is so important that the King James Version mentions the word water over 363 times. There was an interesting scientific experiment conducted a while back: a group of behavioral scientists put a rat in a tank of water. The tank had smooth sides, so that the rats could not escape or rest. The scientist observed the rats to see how long they would survive before drowning. The average time was about 17 minutes. The experiment was then repeated. During the next trial the scientists "rescued" the rats just before the point of drowning. They picked them up out of the tank, dried them off, and returned them to their cage. They fed them and let them play for a few days. The experiment was then repeated again. This time the average survival time for the rats increased. Their survival time increased from 17 minutes to 36 hours. The scientist explained that phenomenon by pointing out that the 2nd time around the rats had hope. They believed that they could survive because they had received a helping hand the first time around.

In *Matthews 14:22-33* Peter was in the midst of a frightening storm. However, we see Peter's step of faith. It's important to note the circumstance that Peter was in because he took some important steps. Like Peter and the disciples in Matthew 14, we often find ourselves in the middle of storms. I will never forget growing up in the little town of Lilesville, N.C. Any time a storm would come up with thunder, lighting, and strong winds, my parents would always tell us to turn off the lights, TV, and radio because God was at work. Over the years I have come to realize what my parents were talking about. It wasn't so much in the natural, but it was in the spiritual. They wanted us to be still and allow the Lord to give us peace or ease the storm.

As you read this book, many of you are dealing with a storm. Maybe, your storm deals with trials and tribulations, heartache and pain, sickness and disease, money crisis, marital conflicts, or maybe you have a stormy relationship with a member of the church. We all have storms in our life. Anyone who tells you that Christianity is a bed of roses doesn't understand the truth of God working in our lives. While it is true that sometimes God does move storms, more often God allows us to go through storms as a teaching tool that shows us that He is a sovereign God and that He has total control of every situation. As we refer back to Matthew notice that it was Jesus fault that the disciples were in the storm. According to this passage and the passage in the Gospel according to Mark, Jesus made or constrained His disciples to get into the ship. The word "constrained" here means that Jesus ordered or commanded His disciples to take the ship across the Sea of Galilee. The disciples were in a storm because Jesus ordered them to go across the sea in the boat. How is it that a God that loves us so much will allow us to go through a storm? The good news is that when the Lord sends us into a storm there is a purpose. Sometimes, it's for spiritual growth. The Lord will use a storm to help us grow and mature in our spiritual walk with Jesus. He will use it to help increase our faith and obedience. Remember what Paul says in **Romans 5:3, "Not only that, but we rejoice in our sufferings knowing that suffering produces endurance." James 1:2-4 says, "Consider it pure joy, my brothers and sisters whenever you face trials of many kinds, because you know that the** *testing of your faith produces. Let perseverance finish its work so that you may be mature and complete, not lacking anything."* I believe that the whole purpose of the storm was to help the disciples grow in their faith. They had to learn to trust God, even when He was not physically present with them. These are the times when you have to walk by faith and not by sight. It doesn't matter what you're going through or how deadly the storm may appear. Keep an attitude of faith. Stay calm. Stay in a positive frame of mind.

Don't try to do it on your own, but keep your faith in God. Always remember, the things you need to survive the storm.

Chapter 3

"THANK GOD FOR WHAT HE DIDN'T DO"

The foundation of this chapter is based upon *II Corinthians 12:7-10*, *"And lest I should be exalted above measure through the abundance of the revelations, there was given to me a thorn in the flesh, the messenger of Satan to buffet me lest I should be exalted above measure. For this thing I besought the Lord thrice, that it might depart from me. And he said unto me. My grace is sufficient for thee" for my strength is made perfect in weakness. Most gladly therefore will I rather in my infirmities, that the power of Christ may rest upon me. Therefore I take pleasure in infirmities, in reproaches, in necessities, in persecutions, in distress for Christ's sake, for when am weak then am I strong."*

Remember the title of this chapter, "Thank God for what He didn't do." This particular statement is an oxymoron. Webster's dictionary defines the word or concept of an oxymoron as a combination of contradictory terms. Examples of an oxymoron are great depression, pretty ugly, walking dead, and running behind. All of these terms are contradictory. There will be times in our lives, as believers, when we will praise God for what He didn't do. Have you ever asked God to move something out of your way and He didn't? Have you asked God to do this great thing in your life and you've prayed and fasted, but you saw it as though it was a mirage. It was so close that you could almost taste it. The stars had aligned themselves just for you and it seemed like God was getting ready to give you the desires of your heart. Then out of nowhere, the thing that you had been asking God for didn't come through. Think back over your life the storms that made you want to give up or give into desperation and despair. The storm that put you on the verge of suicide, made you lose sleep, hair, and almost made you lose your mind. I've learned that it's in this place; the eye of the storm that God will do one of two things: He will either remove the storm or give you strength to get through the storm. In the midst of every storm is where you learn to appreciate the peace of a calm day. Storms are placed in your life to develop you.

As believers, we love to hear stories about answered prayers. We get thrilled about hearing about God's miraculously marvelous interventions and how God made a way out of no way. We want to know how God in His eternal and divine wisdom opened up the windows of Heaven and poured out unimaginable blessings. We all have heard of powerful and prolific testimonies. We love to hear stories about how people were lost in storms and how they were rescued at the final hour. This reminds me of a story that was told to me several years ago when I was going through a storm of my own.

The story was about a young tree. The young tree faced many storms through its life. Storms that was full of powerful winds, torrential rains, famine, ice, and snow. The young tree had to bear all the weight across its immature branches. At times, the young tree questioned its Maker asking, "Why have you let so many storms come into my life?" His Maker whispered, "You will understand one day; stand firm and make it through these storms." The tree continued to plea to its Master. If I go through one more winter, the snow will surely break my branches. If I face any more powerful winds, I will surely be uprooted and moved away. His Maker whispered, "Stand strong, dig your roots deep into the soil, and you will understand someday." Somehow, the young tree kept the positive thoughts in mind and managed to survive. He made it thru, even thru the toughest storms. Even in the rough winds of the toughest storms when things should have broken the young tree down, it found a way to stand firm. As the young tree grew, it became taller and stronger as it matured. The tree realized the storms were not there to break him or to uproot him, but only to make him stronger. We as believers love these powerful stories of how God can make a lasting impression and give a stamp of approval on our lives. It lets us know that our God is more than able to supply all of our needs. But what do you do when it seems like Heaven has flipped the sign closed? You are no longer able to hear from Heaven because it has become silent. What do you do when you ask, plea, and beg, but God does not answer your prayers? What happens when it seems that God is ignoring your clarion call? The Apostle Paul is a great place to begin to find answers to these questions.

    Let's get to know the Apostle Paul. Paul was what most called the 14th apostle. After Judas Iscariot betrayed the Lord and Jesus rose from the dead and ascended to Heaven, the leaders chose an apostle to replace Judas. The replacement had to be someone who had been with the Lord from the time of His baptism until the time of His ascension. Matthias, the 13th apostle, was chosen to take over the apostolic ministry. The Apostle Paul claimed to be an apostle appointed by Jesus on the road to Damascus, thus most consider him the 14th apostle. Paul gives us examples on how to handle storms, failures, and defeat. He did not do it once, but even when he had been down time after time. All of us can learn a lesson from Paul about failure. I am amazed how Paul continued to take a licking and kept on ticking.

Paul says in ***Galatians 2:8-9, "For God, who was at work in Peter as an apostle to the circumcised, was also at work in me as an apostle to the Gentiles James, Cephas and John, those esteemed as pillars, and gave me and Barnabas the right hand of fellowship when they recognized the grace given to me. They agreed that we should go to the Gentiles, and they to the circumcised."*** Paul was circumcised on the 8th day and grew up in the city of Tarsus of Cilicia, a city made up of primarily non-Jews. He was born a Roman citizen, the son of a Pharisee, and educated under a doctor of law Gamaliel. He was a student of Greek and Jewish literature. When we find ourselves going through a storm, we precede to ask God a truck load of questions. Questions like: God, "Why me?" God, "Why do you allow people to hurt and take advantage of me?" or "I've been fasting, praying, walking, and obeying your Word, so why is this happening to me?" I like how William Barclay translates ***II Corinthians 4:8-9 - We are hard pressed*** *on every side, but not crushed; perplexed, but not in despair; persecuted, but not abandoned; struck down, but not destroyed.* He says we are sore pressed at every point, but not hemmed in. We are at our wits end, but never at our hopes end. We are persecuted by men, but never abandoned by God. We are knocked down, but not knocked out. Paul even had physical infirmities that he called his thorn in the flesh. Many scholars have opinions of what Paul was talking about. Some suggest that Paul meant he was home sick and longed to return, which caused him to fall into a state of depression. Others suggest that Paul had gone through a major divorce that caused his heart to be broken. Then there are those that suggest that Paul was dealing with his sexuality or that he was dealing with a disease of the eye that caused him much pain. You and I may never know what Paul's thorn was on this side of Heaven, but Paul clearly states in this chapter when I am weak, then I am strong. Paul gives us encouragement as the people of God on how to deal with failure and hardships in life and still survive the test of time. Paul said, "I prayed three times a day and God still didn't remove his thorn." The key is that he still prayed. The thorn kept him humble. Because even though he had his issues; God was still able to use him, just the way he was. Here is a present day example of how storms can keep us humble and build-up our strength.

Thank God for What He Didn't Do

Well-known basketball legend, Michael Jordan once did a commercial where he walked into an arena where fans were shouting his name "Michael!! Michael!! Michael!!" He then says, "I've missed over 9,000 shots in my career, I've lost over 300 games, and 26 times I've been trusted to take the game winning shot and missed. I've failed over and over again in my life and that's why I have succeeded." Michael Jordan didn't focus on his storms, but he focused on his strengths. Isn't that good news, my brothers and sisters that even in the midst of what you're going through God can still use you? Recognize that even when you have a "thorn" in your flesh or a losing record; you still have the ability to be blessed by God. You have been praying and asking God to please let the storm of life pass you by, but He keeps telling you that His grace is sufficient. In other words, God is simply saying, "I'm enough, all by myself." Always remember, though the storms of life may come and the issues of life challenges the very fiber of our soul, no matter how heavy the burden; God's grace is always enough all by itself.

CHAPTER 4

"I DID SURVIVE"

> *WHO EVER READS THIS I'M IN THE DARK AS I'M WRITING THIS I'M DIEING I'm 28 years-old my name is mike I had to break in your house I took blankets off the couch I have hypothermia I didn't take any thing A wave thru me out of my house down the block I don't think I'm going to make it. The water outside is 10 ft. deep at least Theres no resue Tell my dad I love him and I tryed getting out his number is 111-122-333 his name is Tony. I hope u can read this I'm in the dark I took a black jacket tooo Goodbye. God all mighty help me"*

These were the heartbreaking words of a Hurricane Sandy victim. The note made it around social media including Facebook and Twitter before falling into the hands of a local radio station host. Justin Louis, a Disc Jockey at WOBM Radio, decided to call the number listed on the note. On his second attempt DJ Louis was able to connect with Mike's father, Tony. DJ Louis explained who he was and why he had called. He then mentioned the note. Tony responded with miraculous news. "Yeah that's my son Mike. He's here would you like to talk to him?" DJ Louis was shocked by what he had heard. Mike had survived this incredible battle against Hurricane Sandy. Like Mike, many of us have been in similar situations. We have been in storms when we felt like giving up and writing a letter saying, "Goodbye to our family." But something on the inside of us causes us to have faith in a God that we know is able to deliver us from any type of storm.

This story of survival reminds me of Paul in Acts 27. Paul gives us faith to hold to the hand of an unchangeable God. Faith is not believing that God can, but knowing that God will. Faith is death to doubt, dumb to discouragement, blind to impossibilities, calm to calamity, peace for problems, and triumph to tribulation. Faith only knows success in God. **Now faith is the substance of things hoped for and the evidence of things not seen. (Hebrews 11:1)** Faith is the essence of all outer manifestation of what has yet to be revealed. Faith is the outward sign that God will reveal in the spiritual realm to those who believe on Him.

Paul, the Apostle of Jesus, is sailing under God's direction to Rome. He's in God's perfect will and God's perfect timing. Yet, we see that Paul sailed to Rome not as a pastor, apostle, or an ambassador for God, but as a prisoner. Paul was traveling under arrest. His destination was the Roman prison. He was under constant surveillance by the Roman Centurion. Paul had already forewarned the sailors in ***Acts 27:10, men I can see the voyage is going to be disastrous and bring great loss to the ship and cargo and tour own lives also.*** Not many days after this, there was a great storm. I can imagine that this storm was similar in magnitude to a hurricane in the Mediterranean Sea. In this area it would have been described as a typhoon. In Greek it is known as "tuphon" meaning father of winds or whirlwind. In comparison the typhoon they faced is similar to the hurricanes we face today. A violent storm with thunder, lightning, torrential rain, and gale force winds. They are powerful and disastrous. However, the likelihood of surviving this storm in the sea is very small. This storm is known as the chief plague of sailors because these powerful winds are enough to break their sails and vessels into pieces. The sailors and the ship which (signifies the church) didn't have the strength to fight the storm on their own. They only had one choice and that was to allow the wind to direct the ship. One must understand that the winds in this test are symbolic. They are the Holy Spirit, which guides, directs, and influences the life of the believer. My brothers and sisters understand that there will be storms in your life; whenever, they come you must let go and let God. You must allow the storms of life to run their course. Don't fight against the storm because it will only wear you out. Sometimes, we go through what I like to call spiritual storm surges. A storm surge in the natural is a rise in the ocean level caused by high winds and low pressure of an offshore tropical storm or hurricane. Storm surges hit the coast, as a wall of water, for up to 25 ft. The surges can destroy everything in its path. Often times we are hit with spiritual surges. Reflect back over your life. Recall when Murphy's Law was in full effect in your life. Everything that could go wrong went wrong. Every email and text was bad news. Every conversation was depressing. All you wanted was to drift away like the old Calgon commercial says: "Calgon, just take me away." There are times in every believer's life that you will be hit with an avalanche of agony. You will feel beat down, perplexed, and in worrisome predicaments. Spiritual surges comes when you least expect them. They seem to appear rolling down hills and barreling around curves from behind your blind spot; at the drop of a dime. "No warning" and "No trace" of the coming tragedy. It is just a "BOOM" out of nowhere and then you are faced with a storm in which you are unprepared. I love how James put it in *James 1:2-4 -My brethren, count it all joy when ye fall into divers temptations; Knowing this, that the trying of your faith worketh patience. But let patience have her perfect work, that ye may be perfect and entire, wanting nothing. (KJV)* Wow, that's good news for believers. Knowing that the testing of you faith brings about joy. Think of it like this: it's only a test and Jesus is the master teacher. He grades with a curve. So when you may have failed, you probably should have flunked out of the class and never been allowed back, but Jesus grants you grace. When you are drowning in the floods of life, Jesus comes to your rescue. The Bible says in *Acts 27:17, so the men hoisted it aboard. Then they passed ropes under the ship itself to hold it together. Because they were afraid they would run aground on the sandbars of Syrtis, they lowered the sea anchor and let the ship be driven along.* In this text the sailor represents the members of the church and the ship represents the church, *Ecclesia.* They tied both sides of the ship, so that it might not split and fall into pieces. This is what sailors call frapping. Frapping is done by putting a long rope under the keel and over the gunwale to help the ship stay together. The rope represents faith in God. For without faith it is impossible to please God. This is why the Bible tells us to walk by faith and not by sight. Because when you walk by what you see you are subject to lose your focus. When you walk by sight bills can get you down, relationships can get you depressed, and job situations can make you sad. But when you walk by faith, you realize that trouble doesn't last always. When you walk by faith, you realize that what grandmother said is still true. He may not come when you want Him to, but He is always on time.

In the midst of the storm, Paul stands firm in his faith, which is in Jesus Christ. Paul lets the sailors know we may lose the ship, but we will survive. No matter what you may lose in life you will survive. 276 men were on the ship, but in order for them to survive they had to throw some stuff overboard. There will be times in life that while you are going through your storm you will have to drop that extra baggage and focus totally on the favor and grace of God. They had planned to kill the prisoners on the ship, so that they couldn't escape, but they wanted to spare Paul's life. They allowed the prisoners to swim and those that couldn't swim had to hold onto the broken pieces. The only way that we will ever survive the storms of life is to hold onto the Word of God. We may not be able to quote every Scripture or recall every chapter, but use what you have and God will do the rest.

Chapter 5

"I CAN'T TAKE NO MORE"

Life is composed of pitfalls, potholes, experiences, and encounters. Each experience provides a new challenge to your character. They test your integrity and examine your spirit. Life's greatest wars are not fought on a physical battlefield, but they are fought within the walls of the human mind. Life's most ferocious conflicts are not outer conflicts. The scares that inflict the most permanent damage are not found on the skin. The deepest scars are found in the soul. Life is composed of moments when you question your existence. There are times in your life when you are so confused. You are unsure of where to turn or who to turn to. Situations are shady, people are distant, friends become enemies, and you are lost in the balance. Lost wondering what your purpose is and clueless about how to get closer to it. In these moments you feel alone, desperate, abandoned, and undeserving. You are left with searching for any sign from God to comfort you and reassure you that you are indeed worth it. During the midst of questioning, we face chaos and calamity that leads to heartache, pain, sadness, and sorrow. You begin to talk to yourself and try to figure out how you can handle the storms that have been placed in your life. After you have lived a little and reached a certain level of maturity, you finally realize storms are a natural part of life. Storms in the natural are much like storms in the spiritual. Let's explore the following parallel of natural versus spiritual storms.

Natural storms (hurricanes, typhoons, and tornadoes) are formed when climate is off balance. Likewise, in the spiritual sense the climate in your life may be off balance and is making its way for a spiritual storm to form. Climate is defined as the composite or generally prevailing weather condition of a region. Temperature, air pressure, humidity, precipitation, sunshine, cloudiness, and winds all determine climate. Each condition can add to the development of a specific storm formation. In other words storms can come in different ways, shapes, and sizes. We will all face a storm in our life at one point or another.

I've noticed in studying and observing storms, that they can generally be divided into three types. Each storm type dictates how you will deal with them. The first storm is *"Opposition Storms."* We face this storm, simply by doing what is right. My father gave me a very simple analogy when I was growing up. He said, "Son you can't go wrong going right." To put it another way, these are storms that arise as a result of doing God's will. Have you ever prayed, fasted, and sought God for the person in your life to recover from cancer, but they continued to suffer? Any situations you face in life, you should pray, declare, and decree God's Word. We find a similar scenario in Genesis.

In *Genesis 26* there was a famine in the land that prompted Isaac to move to Egypt. God appeared to him in a dream and told him not to go. God intended to bless Isaac in the land of the famine. Isaac obeyed God and stayed. True to His promise, God blessed him. Often times we are moved by our emotions to leave or abandon the ship in the midst of life's storms. We have been instructed in His Word to remain patient. In *Genesis 26:14-16*, the Philistines grew envious of Isaac's wealth and blessing. They were moved by envy and jealousy that they not only blocked the wells that were vital to his water supply, but also asked him to move away from their land. Potential disaster loomed. There will be times when you are in the will of God, while in the midst of your storm. This is confusing to the enemy because God is still blessing you, as you are going through your storm. Even when everyone on your job is receiving pink slips and you receive a promotion, they can't understand how or why God is still blessing you. It is simply because you are in the will of God. The way you deal with this type of storm is to continue to do what is right. Don't turn and flee in the wrong direction. Continue to do what's right in the eyes of the Lord.

The second type of storm is the *"Opened Door Storm."* In this kind of storm you face a Jonah-type of storm. Jonah, son of Amittai, appears in II Kings as a prophet from Goth-heper that was located a few miles north of Nazareth. Jonah is the central character in the book of Jonah. He was commanded by God to go to the city of Nineveh to prophesy against it. There was great wickedness in Nineveh that had come up before God. Jonah refused and instead tried to flee from the presence of the Lord by going to Joppa and sailing to Tarshish, which geographically, is in the opposite direction. A huge storm arises and the sailors realize that this is no ordinary storm, so they began to cast lots. They discovered that Jonah was to blame. Jonah accepted responsibility and stated that if he is thrown overboard the storm will cease. My brothers and sisters there will be times on this Christian journey that your disobedience will cause storms to come upon your life. Disobedience and sin will breed storms. Sin is a gateway to storms. There is only one way to deal with storms of this type. You have to turn completely around and repent. Repentance is the only way to avoid this kind of storm. The Bible says in ***I John 1:8-9, if we say that we have no sin, we deceive ourselves, and the truth is not in us. If we confess our sins he is faithful and righteous to forgive us of our sins and to cleanse us from all unrighteousness.*** Praying and fasting will not help you with this storm. An increase in your offering will have no effect. Obedience is the only antidote.

The third and final storm is what I like to call *"Life Storms."* Have you ever got into your car and found your engine light on? You're sitting there wondering does this only happen to me? Well I have news for you, it happens to everyone. There are certain hardships that come along that can easily be misunderstood as storms. For example: rebellious children, more bills than you can pay, sudden unemployment, and divorce. All of these are hardships that can be mistaken as storms. The way you deal with these types of storms is with patience and wisdom. Life storms can make you feel like you just can't take anymore. I like how Haruki Murakami puts it: "Sometimes the hardest storms to get through are the ones your soul needs the most." Once the storm is over, you won't remember how you survived the storm, but you did. One thing is certain, when you come out of this storm you won't be the same person who walked in. That's what storms are all about. Today, many preach and teach quick steps that tell Christians if you follow Jesus you will never have to face any challenges or changes. That wasn't true for Jesus and it is not true for anyone else. Following Jesus doesn't offer a monopoly or immunity from storms. What it does do is give us the opportunity to have Jesus in the midst of our troubles. Life comes with trouble. From the time you were born and received your first slap on the bottom your life was destined to be filled with storms. Life on earth is filled with storms. While you and I pursue our God given dreams we will encounter many storms. We can become so burdened that we will feel as though we can't take anymore. When faced with trouble we need to remember what Jesus said in ***John 16:33***, *"**I have told you these things, so that in me you may have {perfect} peace and confidence. In the world you have tribulation and trials and distress and frustration; but be of good cheer for I have overcome the world.**"* Many people give up and abort their God given talents because of the storms that come their way. Never give up, but continue to keep pressing. God is not slack concerning His promise towards you. With every storm you face, you will grow and mature. You will develop as you continue on life's journey. It has often been said, that "what didn't kill you only makes you stronger." When you feel like you can't take it anymore, know that Jesus has the power to carry you through any storm that you may face. This reminds me of a story of strength and faith through the eyes of a child.

There was a little girl whom had lost her parents. She now lived with her grandparents. Her grandparents were up in age and had fallen ill. They had no food in the house, no wood for the stove, and no heat to warm the home. Each morning the little girl woke up early with much hope in her mind. She would get her pen and paper and start to write a prayer to Jesus. In the prayer she told Him all about her problems. She took the letter and placed it in the mailbox. When the mailman came by he saw the letter, but noticed it did not have a stamp. He opened the letter and started to read. He was moved by the little girl's prayer and began to cry. Tears began to roll down his cheeks. The mailman knew he had to help. He knew a doctor that could help heal her grandparents. He knew the grocery man to get food. He knew a carpenter that could gather some wood. That evening when the little girl was on her way home she saw smoke coming from the chimney. She could smell food cooking. She heard her grandparents praising God.

In that moment this little girl picked up another pen and paper and starting writing again.

Her grandmother said, "Child what are you doing?" The little girl replied, "I think I should write a letter to God and say thank you." Even when you think that you can't bear another storm, God will always make provisions and see you through.

Chapter 6

"I AM AN EAGLE"

There are stories told about eagles and their ability to cope with storms. The eagle is known for their size, strength, powers of flight, and vision. Eagles know when storms are approaching long before they even break. Before the storm comes, an eagle will fly to a high point to wait for the winds to calm. When the storm begins to rage the eagle is able to soar powerfully above it. It does not escape the storm; it simply uses its elements to elevate itself through the storm. Like the eagle, when storms come to us we can rise above them by setting our minds and our belief in our Heavenly Father. If we have faith and believe He will strengthen us to weather the storms. Faith will help you weather storms that bring sickness, tragedy, failure, and disappointment. It is not the burdens of life that weighs us down, but it's how we handle them. The Bible says in **Isaiah 40:31, those who hope is in the Lord will renew their strength. They will soar on wings like eagles.** This is a remarkable and amazing lesson for the people of God to learn how the eagle approaches storms. When the storms of life come, they actually help us in our walk of faith. Storms are a part of our lives and they help build us up. When eagles fly above storms, they are actually overcoming them. This is done in a most interesting way. The eagle uses the strength of the storm to rise above it. So, the next time a storm comes your way don't focus on the cloud, but focus on the sunshine that will come after the storm. The interesting thing about storms is that they don't last always. In due time and in due season God will allow the storm to pass. That is one of the things God wants us to know. We can use adversity for our gain. We need to learn from trials, grow from experiences, and be made better. There will be times in life when we will escape trials, flee from trials, and times when trials are to be confronted and endured. We must face the things that challenge us to grow in virtue because storms will come our way. This reminds me of a story by Nancy Missler.

    There was a wounded eagle that was rescued by a kind farmer. The farmer found the bird in one of his fields. He took the bird home, nursed its wounds, and placed him outside in the barnyard to recover. Strangely enough the young eagle soon adapted to the habits of all the barnyard chickens. He learned to walk and cluck like chickens. He learned to drink from a trough and peck the dirt for food. For many years he peacefully resigned himself to his new life on the ground. But then one day one of the farmer's friends spotted the eagle and asked, "Why in the world is that eagle acting like a chicken?" The farmer explained to his friend what had happened to the eagle. The man could hardly accept the farmer's response. "It's just not right," said the friend. The Creator made that kind to soar in the Heavens and not scavenges in the barnyard. One day, the friend picked up the unsuspecting eagle, climbed onto a nearby fence post, and tossed him into the air. The confused bird just fell back to earth and searched for his feathered friends. The man then grabbed the eagle and climbed to the top of the barn. He heaved the bird into the air. Shaken and confused the bird made a few halfhearted flaps before falling into a bale of hay. After shaking his head a few times, the eagle then made himself comfortable and began pecking at the pieces of straw. The friend went home that night dejected. He could barely sleep as he remembered the sight of those powerful talons packed with barnyard mud. He couldn't bear the thought, so the very next day he headed back to the farm for another try. This time he carried the eagle to the top of a nearby mountain where the sky unfolded in a limitless horizon. He looked into the eagles eyes and cried out, "Don't you understand? You weren't made to live with chickens. Why would you want to stay down here when you were born for the sky?" The man held the confused bird making sure the eagle was facing into the brilliant light of the setting sun. He then powerfully heaved the bird into the sky. This time the eagle opened up his wings, looked at the sun, and caught the undrafted rising from the valley and disappeared into the clouds of Heaven.

God's children were born to fly. They were created by a loving God to soar. He has called us to live in the heights, yet too many of us have huddled together in the barnyard. We have become content and comfortable with crumbs. The enemy wants us to be disturbed by the sight of the lightening and moved by the sound of the thunder that accompanies storms. The enemy's strategy is to get your perspective turned upside down, so that you will become helpless when facing your problems. There are three things the enemy wants you to believe that are not true. The first lie Satan wants you to believe is that the storm you are facing is permanent. When you are in the middle of a hurricane it is easy to think that it will never end. Most tornados only last about 10 minutes or less, but it could seem like a lifetime. Once, we start to think this way we lose hope and give up. We throw in the towel. Don't allow yourself to do this. Yes, storms are a fact of life, but another fact of life is that they always pass. Just remember that not too far over the horizon, lies the blue sky. Hang in there. You will soon see the beautiful rainbow. We are not destined to be destroyed by water. Hold onto your hope in Jesus Christ.

The second lie he wants us to believe is that the problem is much bigger than it appears. Rearview mirrors often read "objects may be closer than they appear." You can blot out the moon with your thumb, but we all know the moon is larger than our thumb. The wrong perspective can convince us of something that isn't true. Consider this, the next time you are going through a storm step back and try to see it from God's perspective. Once you do this, you will suddenly see how tiny the storm really is compared to the immense greatness of God. Don't trust your eyesight. The Bible has cautioned us to walk by faith and not by sight. When you walk by what you see you are subject to lose your focus and your faith. Oh!! But when you walk by faith you learn that all things are working for your good.

The third lie is that you can fix this. Have you ever been in the midst of a crisis; fretting, worrying, and then suddenly realize that you haven't asked God for help? The enemy wants you to focus all your attention on the problem, so that you forget about the solution. Most believers never take advantage of God's abundant resources. *Ephesians 3:20 says, in the amplified version ,God is able to do superabundantly far over and above all that we dare ask or think, beyond our highest prayer, desires, thoughts, hopes, or dreams. Matthew 9:29 says, according to your faith, it will be done to you.* Therefore, the key to unlock all that God wants for you in your life is really faith. There are two ways to approach life. You can choose to live by faith or by fear. You can be an optimist or a pessimist. You can choose to win or lose. You can choose to soar above your storms, by catching the wind.

CHAPTER 7

"DON'T EVER GIVE UP"

I was raised in a wonderful Christian home with great values and morals. Every Sunday evening, my father would gather us around the floor model T.V at 8:00 pm. to watch the Evangelist Jimmy Swaggart. Many times the T.V. would be turned off and we would just sit, while reading the Bible. We would pray and read our Sunday school lesson. But now, instead of sitting with my family around the television; I am sitting in the Middle East, in the middle of a war. I am in the middle of things that I did not ask for, could never have imagined, and will never forget.

I was a 20-year-old young man and a soldier at war. I was assigned to serve in Desert Storm. I had enlisted in the United States Navy on July 5, 1988. My position was a Hospital Corpsman. I had spent all of my time with the U.S. Marine Corps and trained at Camp Pendleton with the 3rd Battalion. I was in the United States Navy and had never been on a ship. I was in a foreign country, in which others would have taken as a vacation, but I was in the midst of a war. I must admit for the first time in my life I was scared to death. I was told that once I hit the beach, my life expectancy would be about 20 seconds. I can't remember of any night that I had a full night's rest. Every day I could hear the air raid and the wailing sound of sirens. I am still haunted by the sound even now. It rings in my ears to this very day; seemingly louder and more intense each time. I can recall the day I was called to the operating room of a triage unit to assist with surgery. As I was standing in the operating room, I suddenly realized that I was standing in some type of liquid. Unsure of what it was, I looked down and was shocked, that I was standing in a pool of a young soldier's blood. There before me was a recently married, 18-year-old man that had lost both legs, his left side torn apart, and he lost his arm. I felt closeness to him because he was from my home state of North Carolina. During that moment, still photographs of my life flashed before my eyes. Why was all of this happening to me? How could I be in this awful place? Then it dawned on me, that everything that I had learned growing up in my Christian home and the training that I received in the Baptist Church began to come back to my mind. Thoughts of me not making it out of the war and never seeing my family again quickly vanished. That was one of the many events that I have encountered in my life; however, all of them have resulted in a lesson.

God has a purpose in everything that you go through. God uses the things that we go through as teaching tools. Every lesson is filled with faith nuggets. It was Paul that stated in ***Philippians 1:6, "Being confident of this, that he who began a good work in you will carry it on to completion until the day of Jesus Christ."*** Before I go any further I need to tell you that every promise comes with a price. There is no victory without a fight. There is no testimony without a test. There is no crown without a cross. There is no resurrection without a crucifixion. There are just things you have to go through to get to your promise. My years in the military were part of a process. Those days in the desert taught me how to lean and totally depend upon Jesus. My faith in the Maker, the Creator of all humanity was increased through that process. I had faithfully served my country and my years of service were complete. The next chapter of my life would begin just five short years later.

In June of 1993, I accepted my call to the Gospel ministry. Less than a year later I was blessed to pastor my first church, Morning Star Baptist

Church in Charlotte, North Carolina. I was the youngest pastor in the city at that time. Shortly after my installation, I was married. I was a new pastor, a new husband, and now a new dad. My first son, Tobias Wall II was on his way. Another process of growth began in my life. As a child growing up, I saw a wonderful relationship between my parents, so it was my impression that if I followed their blueprint for marriage; I would have the same success. That was not so, at all. We were both very young and lacked maturity. We were not meeting each other's needs. During this challenge in my life, I was devastated. One day, I was the rising star of the east and the brightest star shinning, but just in 2 ½ years into pastoring and marriage, I was suffering through a divorce. I was a pastor that was preaching and teaching the Word of God, but going through a divorce. How could this be happening to me? My father was a pastor and my mother was the head of the Missionary Department. They gave me every foundation to succeed, yet I was facing a storm that almost caused me to lose my mind. In a blink of an eye, I went from living in a house that was built for our young family, to living in a cold, lonely room at the Continental Inn Hotel that was in a not so pleasant part of the city. I had nothing. I slept in my car and only had one suit, so I could arrive at church early to get dressed. I use to put on my robe, so that the congregation would not notice that

I wore the same shoes and suit every Sunday. In all reality, I was homeless and I felt a sense of helplessness. I'd been preaching and pouring my heart out, yet I felt like God was ignoring me. I felt like, He who had called me to do His will had turned His back on me. I truly understood what David felt like in Psalms.

Psalms 22:1 David asks, "My God, my God why hast thou forsaken me? Why are thou so far from the words of my groaning?" In this particular Psalm, David is crying out to God, not only because he feels alone, but it is a cry to God who got him in this mess in the first place and now David feels as though God has gone "AWOL" (Absent Without Leave- a military term that means you left without permission) on his situation. He felt that God had fallen asleep on his situation. David was going through one of the most tragic times in his life. This Psalm is a cry for deliverance from something he never would have been in, if he hadn't been following God. Isn't it amazing that sometimes it appears that when you are following God, you are in more of a mess than you were before you decided to follow God's will, God's purpose, or God's plan? Isn't it amazing that sometimes, when you follow God, that you question yourself to the fact of, "why in the world am I following You?" The thing about the whole deal is where you end up is not where you thought you were going towards. In

Psalms 22 when David asks, "Why hast thou forsaken me?" He is not talking about the absence or the presence of God. When he says, "God, you've forsaken me." David is talking about the activity of God. The Spirit of the text suggests that David is confessing to God that he feels God is ignoring him. The reason that David felt like God was ignoring him was because he didn't see anything happening on the exterior of his life. This is the war between the flesh and the spirit. The war between what the spirit knows and what the flesh has to see and feel. David acknowledges that if God is not responding to his prayer request then God is ignoring him. So David suggested that if God is not doing anything, then God is up to nothing. When you talk about the flesh versus the spirit, the spirit goes on the basis of what you know. The flesh goes on the basis of what you feel. I must be transparent that there were times in ministry when I really felt like walking away. I use to receive calls from my co-labors, but they stopped, invitations to preach the Word of God suddenly stopped and were cancelled. I was told things like they didn't check their calendar. I felt like I had been exiled to the Island of Patmos. Friends that I grew up with no longer cared, family members began to reject me, and church folk held private meetings to plot and scheme to put me out. Deacons and trusted confidantes of the Ministry suggested that maybe I needed to sit down and wait for the storm to blow over. I couldn't sit. I had a call on my life to preach the Gospel. I began to preach like Heaven and earth were coming together. I've learned valuable lessons through my storms. I've learned to follow the example of the eagle and rise above what I was going through. The Bible says, in ***Ecclesiastes 3, "For everything there is a season and a time for every purpose under heaven."***

    I challenge you to remember that no matter what you may go through, rise above it and soar like the eagle. God would never allow you to come this far to lose. The choice is yours; you can peck with the chickens or soar with the eagles. For me, I choose to soar. It has been 18 years later and God has blessed me and allowed me to pastor the greatest ministry on this side of Heaven. I have been assigned the awesome task by God to be the Senior Pastor at Olive Branch Missionary Baptist Church.

    If I had to change one storm in my life, I wouldn't. It was in the midst of my storms that I learned some of the greatest lessons in my life. If you are faithful to God, He will be faithful to you. As you face your next trial, keep your eyes on the only one who will carry you through. He's already at work right now guiding, leading, directing, and providing for you every step of the way. When the next storm hits, you have to know that you have everything you need to not only survive the storm, but come out victorious through the storm.

IF THE ENEMY KNEW WHAT I WOULD BECOME AFTER THE STORM, HE WOULD HAVE LEFT ME ALONE.

BUILDING WITH A STORM IN MIND

FAITH TO SURVIVE

FOREWORD BY JOHN H. WALKER

TOBIAS M. WALL

ABOUT THE AUTHOR
TOBIAS M. WALL

A native of Lilesville, North Carolina, Tobias M. Wall is one of three children born to the late Rev. Wall and Mrs. Doris Wall-Marshall. He was raised in a Christian home with his siblings Phyllis and Theo. He is the father of four and is an ever present force in their lives teaching by example.
He attended high school at Anson Senior High school in Wadesboro, NC. Following graduation from High School he entered the United States Navy where he served for 4 years until 1992. He continued enhancing his education beginning a decade long quest in Biblical studies at New Life University, (ITC) Inter-denominational Theological Center, and Shaw University; he culminated his educational aspirations by obtaining a B.S in Biblical Studies in 2001 at Queen City Bible College.

After God placed an anointed calling on his life he began his Pastoring career more than 20 years ago and continues to educate himself daily. He has pastored in the Mecklenburg and Union County areas of North Carolina, he has been summoned to bring forth the gospel all across the country. Since 2005 he has been the visionary of Olive Branch Missionary Baptist Church located in Marshville, North Carolina.

He is an entrepreneur..... he founded, owned, and operated The Knott Shoppe a clothing boutique for men, specializing in custom fit apparel and accessories.

He is an author....the author of "Pastor's most Inspiring Scriptures" a collection of scriptures taken from the word of God to empower people to align their lives with the vision that God has for them.

His current book "Building with a Storm in mind" the second of three books that he has pinned. This book takes a close look at the storms people face in life and gives encouragement to build their faith based on Biblical examples and true life stories of those whom overcame their storms.

He is the Founder of T.M. Wall Ministries a Community Enhancement Leadership Initiative based out of North Carolina to sponsor leadership and betterment for the people in the surrounding area.

Educated, strong, and spiritually grounded he proves that great men of God continue to thrive even when the odds are stacked against you. Tobias M. Wall is an awesome man of God, a magnificent teacher, and a dynamic preacher who is always excited about sharing the news the good news of God to uplift people.

Is there a book inside of you? Ever wanted to self publish but didn't know how? Concerned about the financial part of self publishing? Relax. Take a deep breath. We can help!

Finally! An affordable Self Publishing company for all of your Self Publishing needs. We have the right services, with the right prices with the right quality. So, what are you waiting for?

Unpack those dreams, break out that pen, your dreams of getting published may not be so far off after all!

Jasher Press & Co. is here to provide you with Consulting, Book Formatting, Cover Designs, editing services but most importantly inspiration to bring your dreams to past.

And this whole process can be done in less than 90 days! You thought about it, you talked about it but now is the time!

WWW.JASHERPRESS.COM
1-888-220-2068
CUSTOMERSERVICE@JASHERPRESS.COM

Made in the USA
Columbia, SC
02 May 2025

57469871R00046